LOW FODMAP AIR FRYER COOKBOOK

DR. JESSICA SMITH

TABLE OF CONTENTS

CHAPTER ONE

How to Use this Cookbook

Choose Your Recipe: Start by selecting a recipe from this cookbook that fits your dietary needs and preferences.

Review Ingredients: Check all the ingredients listed in the recipe to ensure they comply with the low FODMAP diet and that you have everything you need.

Prep Ingredients: Prepare your ingredients as specified in the recipe. This might include washing, cutting, and measuring.

Adjust Settings: Preheat your air fryer as recommended. Adjust the cooking temperature and timer according to the recipe instructions.

Cook in Batches: If the recipe requires it, cook in batches to avoid overcrowding the air fryer basket. This ensures even cooking.

Shake or Flip: For even cooking and browning, shake the basket or flip the items halfway through cooking, if the recipe advises it.

Check Doneness: Ensure food is cooked thoroughly by checking its internal temperature with a food thermometer or ensuring its visual appeal and texture are as described.

Rest: Let the food rest for a few minutes after cooking if required. This step is important for dishes like meats that need time to redistribute juices.

Garnish and Serve: Add any recommended garnishes before serving to enhance flavor and presentation.

Clean Up: After cooking, clean the air fryer according to the manufacturer's instructions to maintain its performance and longevity.

Understanding Low Fodmap Air Fryer

The Low FODMAP diet is a dietary approach primarily used to manage symptoms of irritable bowel syndrome (IBS) and other digestive disorders.

FODMAPs, an acronym for Fermentable Oligosaccharides, Disaccharides, Monosaccharides, and Polyols, are short-chain carbohydrates that are poorly absorbed in the small intestine and can cause digestive discomfort in sensitive individuals.

The diet involves a process of eliminating high FODMAP foods, which can trigger symptoms like bloating, gas, and abdominal pain.

Using a Low FODMAP Air Fryer Cookbook integrates this dietary approach with the convenience and health benefits of air frying.

Air fryers use hot air to cook food, requiring minimal oil, which can be beneficial for those needing a low-fat option alongside their low FODMAP requirements.

The cookbook provides recipes specifically formulated to avoid high FODMAP ingredients while delivering delicious, crispy results typical of traditional frying.

Understanding how to utilize a Low FODMAP Air Fryer Cookbook involves recognizing suitable ingredients, adapting traditional frying recipes to low FODMAP alternatives, and managing portion sizes to maintain compliance with the diet.

This method allows individuals sensitive to FODMAPs to enjoy a broader range of foods without experiencing discomfort, using an appliance that offers a healthier cooking method.

Benefits of Low Fodmap Air Fryer

Using a Low FODMAP Air Fryer offers multiple benefits, particularly for individuals managing digestive health issues like IBS.

The Low FODMAP diet reduces intake of certain carbohydrates that can cause intestinal discomfort, while an air fryer provides a healthier cooking method by minimizing the use of cooking oils.

Firstly, air frying significantly cuts down on the amount of fat compared to traditional frying methods.

This reduction in oil not only helps in managing overall calorie intake but also benefits those who experience worsened digestive symptoms with high-fat meals. For people on a Low FODMAP diet, this means enjoying a wider variety of foods, including traditionally fried dishes, without the discomfort that can come from excessive fat.

Secondly, the use of an air fryer in preparing Low FODMAP meals adds convenience and simplicity. It allows for quick cooking times and easy cleanup, making dietary compliance more manageable and less time-consuming. This can be especially beneficial for individuals with busy schedules who might otherwise find it challenging to prepare Low FODMAP meals consistently.

Lastly, the crisp texture and flavor enhancement provided by air frying can make Low FODMAP meals more appealing.

This can significantly improve meal satisfaction and help individuals stick to the dietary restrictions necessary for managing their symptoms, thereby promoting a better quality of life.

Guidelines for Low Fodmap Air Fryer

When using a Low FODMAP Air Fryer, following specific guidelines can help ensure that meals are both delicious and compliant with dietary needs.

These guidelines are designed to maximize the benefits of both low FODMAP eating and air frying technology.

Ingredient Selection: Focus on using ingredients that are Low FODMAP certified or recognized. Common safe choices include carrots, potatoes, rice, meats, and certain fruits like strawberries and grapes.

Avoid foods high in FODMAPs such as onions, garlic, and wheat-based products.

Portion Control: Even Low FODMAP ingredients can become problematic in large quantities. Stick to recommended serving sizes to keep FODMAP levels within a range that minimizes symptoms.

Cooking Times and Temperatures: Air fryers cook food differently than traditional methods. Refer to the Low FODMAP Air Fryer Cookbook for specific temperatures and times to ensure food is cooked thoroughly without becoming overly dry or burnt.

Cross-Contamination: If sharing an air fryer with others who are not following a Low FODMAP diet, clean it thoroughly between uses to avoid cross-contamination with high FODMAP foods.

Experiment and Adapt: Use the air fryer to experiment with different herbs and spices that are Low FODMAP friendly, such as ginger and turmeric, to enhance flavor without adding irritants.

CHAPTER TWO

Low FODMAP Airfryer Breakfast Recipes

1: Low FODMAP Air Fryer Breakfast Potatoes

Ingredients:

- 2 large russet potatoes, peeled and diced
- 1 tablespoon garlic-infused olive oil
- 1 teaspoon smoked paprika
- 1 teaspoon dried oregano
- Salt and pepper, to taste
- Fresh chives, chopped for garnish

Instructions:

- Preheat your air fryer to 390°F (200°C).
- Toss the diced potatoes with garlic-infused olive oil, smoked paprika, oregano, salt, and pepper in a bowl.
- Spread the potatoes evenly in the air fryer basket. Cook for 20-25 minutes, shaking the basket halfway through, until potatoes are golden and crispy.
- Serve hot, garnished with fresh chives.

Health Benefits:

- Potatoes are a good source of potassium and vitamin C, which are essential for heart health and immunity.
- Using garlic-infused olive oil provides flavor without adding high FODMAP ingredients, making this dish suitable for a sensitive digestive system.

Preparation Time: 30 minutes

2: Low FODMAP Air Fryer Banana Pancakes

Ingredients:

- 2 ripe bananas, mashed
- 2 eggs
- 1/2 cup gluten-free flour
- 1/2 teaspoon baking powder
- 1/4 cup almond milk
- 1 teaspoon vanilla extract
- Maple syrup (for serving)
- Fresh blueberries (for garnish)

Instructions:

- In a large bowl, combine mashed bananas, eggs, gluten-free flour, baking powder, almond milk, and vanilla extract. Stir until the batter is smooth.
- Preheat your air fryer to 350°F (175°C) and line the basket with parchment paper.
- Spoon the batter onto the parchment paper, forming small pancakes.
- Cook for 6-8 minutes or until the pancakes are firm and lightly golden. Flip halfway through cooking for even browning.
- Serve warm with maple syrup and garnish with fresh blueberries.

Health Benefits:

- Bananas provide a rich source of fiber and potassium, while eggs offer high-quality protein and essential nutrients, supporting muscle function and overall health.
- Gluten-free flour makes this dish suitable for those with gluten intolerance or celiac disease.

Preparation Time: 20 minutes

3: Low FODMAP Air Fryer Spinach and Feta Omelette

Ingredients:

- 2 large eggs
- 1/2 cup chopped spinach (fresh or frozen and thawed)
- 1/4 cup crumbled feta cheese (lactose-free if needed)
- Salt and pepper, to taste
- A drizzle of olive oil (for greasing)

Instructions:

- In a bowl, beat the eggs with salt and pepper.
- Mix in the chopped spinach and crumbled feta cheese until well combined.
- Grease the air fryer basket with a little olive oil to prevent sticking.
- Pour the egg mixture into the air fryer basket.
- Cook at 360°F (182°C) for about 8-10 minutes or until the eggs are set and slightly golden on top.
- Carefully remove from the air fryer and serve warm.

Health Benefits:

- Eggs are a great source of protein and vitamins such as B2 and B12, which are essential for energy metabolism and nerve health.
- Spinach adds fiber, iron, and magnesium, while feta provides a tasty, lower lactose option for added calcium without the digestive discomfort.

Preparation Time: 15 minutes

4: Low FODMAP Air Fryer Berry Muffins

Ingredients:

- 1 1/2 cups gluten-free flour
- 1/2 cup granulated sugar
- 1/2 teaspoon baking powder
- 1/4 cup melted butter (lactose-free if needed)
- 2/3 cup lactose-free milk
- 1 teaspoon vanilla extract
- 1 cup mixed berries (such as blueberries and raspberries)

Instructions:

- In a mixing bowl, combine the gluten-free flour, sugar, and baking powder.
- Add in the melted butter, lactose-free milk, and vanilla extract. Mix until smooth.
- Gently fold the mixed berries into the batter.
- Spoon the batter into silicone muffin cups and place them in the air fryer basket.
- Cook at 320°F (160°C) for about 12-15 minutes or until a toothpick inserted into the center of a muffin comes out clean.
- Allow to cool slightly before serving.

Health Benefits:

- These muffins offer a good balance of carbohydrates and fats, suitable for a low FODMAP diet.
- The use of lactose-free ingredients helps avoid digestive issues, while berries provide antioxidants and vitamins without adding excessive sugar.

Preparation Time: 30 minutes

5: Low FODMAP Air Fryer Hash Browns

Ingredients:

- 2 large potatoes, peeled and grated
- 1 tablespoon garlic-infused olive oil
- Salt and pepper, to taste
- Optional: chopped fresh chives or parsley for garnish

Instructions:

- Rinse the grated potatoes in cold water and squeeze out as much moisture as possible using a clean towel.
- Toss the dried grated potatoes with garlic-infused olive oil, salt, and pepper.
- Preheat the air fryer to 400°F (200°C).
- Place the potato mixture in the air fryer basket, spreading evenly.
- Cook for 15-20 minutes, shaking the basket halfway through, until the hash browns are crispy and golden brown.
- Garnish with chopped chives or parsley before serving.

Health Benefits:

- Potatoes are a good source of potassium, which can help maintain normal blood pressure.
- The garlic-infused oil adds flavor without the high FODMAPs found in whole garlic, making it a suitable option for those with digestive sensitivities.

Preparation Time: 25 minutes

6: Low FODMAP Air Fryer Carrot and Zucchini Fritters

Ingredients:

- 1 medium zucchini, grated
- 2 medium carrots, grated
- 1/2 cup gluten-free flour
- 1 teaspoon baking powder
- 2 large eggs, beaten
- Salt and pepper, to taste
- Olive oil spray for cooking

Instructions:

- Mix the grated zucchini and carrots in a colander, sprinkle with a little salt, and let sit for 10 minutes to draw out moisture. Squeeze out the excess water.
- In a bowl, combine the gluten-free flour, baking powder, beaten eggs, salt, and pepper. Add the dried vegetables and stir until well combined.
- Preheat the air fryer to 360°F (182°C) and spray the basket with olive oil.
- Spoon portions of the fritter mixture into the basket, flattening them slightly.
- Cook for 10-12 minutes, flipping halfway through, until the fritters are golden and crispy.
- Serve warm.

Health Benefits:

- Carrots and zucchini are low in FODMAPs and rich in vitamins A and C, which support immune function and skin health.
- These fritters provide a good mix of vegetables and protein, making them a balanced breakfast option.

21

Preparation Time: 30 minutes

7: Low FODMAP Air Fryer Quinoa and Spinach Cakes

Ingredients:

- 1 cup cooked quinoa (cooled)
- 1/2 cup chopped spinach (fresh or frozen and thawed)
- 2 eggs
- 1/4 cup grated Parmesan cheese (low-lactose option)
- Salt and pepper, to taste
- A pinch of smoked paprika
- Olive oil spray for cooking

Instructions:

- In a large bowl, combine the cooked quinoa, chopped spinach, eggs, Parmesan cheese, salt, pepper, and smoked paprika. Mix until well combined.
- Preheat the air fryer to 360°F (182°C) and spray the basket with olive oil.

- Form the mixture into small patties and place them in the air fryer basket. Ensure they don't touch to allow for even cooking.
- Cook for about 15 minutes, turning halfway through, until the patties are golden and firm.
- Serve warm with a side of low FODMAP salsa or a dollop of lactose-free yogurt.

Health Benefits:

- Quinoa is a complete protein source, providing all nine essential amino acids necessary for good health. Spinach adds fiber, iron, and vitamins A and C. T
- his recipe is great for energy support and maintaining digestive health due to its balanced nutritional profile and low FODMAP ingredients.

Preparation Time: 25 minutes

8: Low FODMAP Air Fryer Turkey Breakfast Sausage Patties

Ingredients:

- 1 pound ground turkey
- 1 teaspoon dried sage

- 1/2 teaspoon dried thyme
- 1/2 teaspoon fennel seeds, crushed
- 1/4 teaspoon paprika
- 1/4 teaspoon pepper
- Salt to taste
- Olive oil spray for cooking

Instructions:

- In a bowl, mix the ground turkey with sage, thyme, crushed fennel seeds, paprika, pepper, and salt until well combined.
- Form the mixture into small, flat patties.
- Preheat the air fryer to 380°F (193°C) and lightly spray the basket with olive oil.
- Place the patties in the air fryer basket, ensuring they do not overlap.
- Cook for 10-12 minutes, flipping halfway through, until the patties are fully cooked and have a nice exterior crust.
- Serve hot with a side of low FODMAP-friendly ketchup or mustard.

Health Benefits:

- Turkey is a low-fat protein source that helps maintain muscle mass and keeps you feeling full longer.
- The herbs used add flavor without the need for high FODMAP ingredients, making these patties a safe choice for those managing digestive sensitivities.

Preparation Time: 20 minutes

9: Low FODMAP Air Fryer Cinnamon French Toast Sticks

Ingredients:

- 4 slices gluten-free bread, cut into strips
- 2 eggs
- 1/2 cup lactose-free milk
- 1/2 teaspoon cinnamon
- 1 teaspoon vanilla extract
- Maple syrup for serving
- Olive oil spray for cooking

Instructions:

- In a shallow dish, whisk together the eggs, lactose-free milk, cinnamon, and vanilla extract.
- Dip each bread strip into the egg mixture, allowing it to soak up the liquid for a few seconds.
- Preheat the air fryer to 360°F (182°C) and lightly spray the basket with olive oil.
- Place the soaked bread strips in the basket, making sure they don't overlap.
- Cook for 8-10 minutes, flipping halfway through, until the French toast sticks are golden brown and crispy.
- Serve warm with maple syrup.

Health Benefits:

- This recipe offers a source of protein from the eggs and is gentle on the stomach with lactose-free milk and gluten-free bread.
- Cinnamon helps control blood sugar levels, making it a healthy addition.

Preparation Time: 20 minutes

10: Low FODMAP Air Fryer Sweet Potato Hash

Ingredients:

- 2 medium sweet potatoes, peeled and diced
- 1 red bell pepper, diced (optional, if tolerated)
- 1 tablespoon garlic-infused olive oil
- Salt and pepper, to taste
- Fresh herbs for garnish (such as parsley or cilantro)

Instructions:

- In a bowl, toss the diced sweet potatoes and red bell pepper with garlic-infused olive oil, salt, and pepper.
- Preheat the air fryer to 400°F (204°C).
- Spread the sweet potato mixture evenly in the air fryer basket.
- Cook for 15-20 minutes, stirring halfway through, until the sweet potatoes are tender and lightly browned.
- Garnish with fresh herbs before serving.

Health Benefits:

- Sweet potatoes are a rich source of fiber, vitamins A and C, and antioxidants, which support immune function and gut health.
- The use of garlic-infused oil adds flavor without adding high FODMAP ingredients, making this meal both delicious and digestible.

Preparation Time: 25 minutes

Low FODMAP Airfryer Lunch Recipes

1: Low FODMAP Air Fryer Lemon Herb Chicken

Ingredients:

- 4 boneless, skinless chicken breasts
- 2 tablespoons garlic-infused olive oil
- Juice of 1 lemon
- 1 teaspoon dried oregano
- 1 teaspoon dried basil
- Salt and pepper, to taste
- Lemon slices, for garnish

Instructions:

- In a bowl, mix the garlic-infused olive oil, lemon juice, oregano, basil, salt, and pepper.
- Place the chicken breasts in the mixture, ensuring they are well coated. Let marinate for at least 15 minutes (or up to 2 hours in the refrigerator for more flavor).
- Preheat the air fryer to 360°F (182°C).
- Place the chicken breasts in the air fryer basket and cook for 20-22 minutes, or until the internal temperature reaches 165°F (74°C), turning halfway through cooking.
- Serve the chicken with fresh lemon slices on top.

Health Benefits:

- This recipe provides a high-protein meal with minimal fats, which is great for muscle maintenance and satiety.
- Lemon and herbs not only add flavor without excess calories but also offer vitamins and antioxidants, which support immune health and digestion.

Preparation Time: 30 minutes (including marinating time)

2: Low FODMAP Air Fryer Salmon and Asparagus

Ingredients:

- 4 salmon fillets (about 6 ounces each)
- 1 bunch of asparagus, trimmed
- 2 tablespoons garlic-infused olive oil
- Salt and pepper, to taste
- Lemon wedges, for serving

Instructions:

- Brush each salmon fillet and asparagus with garlic-infused olive oil. Season with salt and pepper.
- Preheat the air fryer to 400°F (204°C).
- Arrange the salmon fillets and asparagus in the air fryer basket in a single layer. You may need to cook in batches depending on the size of your air fryer.
- Cook for 10-12 minutes, or until the salmon is cooked through and flakes easily with a fork.
- Serve immediately with lemon wedges.

Health Benefits:

- Salmon is rich in omega-3 fatty acids, which are crucial for cardiovascular health and reducing inflammation.
- Asparagus is a low FODMAP vegetable that provides fiber, folate, and vitamins A, C, and K.
- This meal is balanced in nutrients, supporting overall health while being easy on digestion.

Preparation Time: 20 minutes

3: Low FODMAP Air Fryer Turkey Burgers

Ingredients:

- 1-pound ground turkey
- 1/4 cup chopped green onions (green parts only)
- 1 teaspoon dried parsley
- 1 teaspoon dried chives
- Salt and pepper, to taste
- 4 gluten-free hamburger buns
- Lettuce, tomato slices, and mustard for serving

Instructions:

- In a bowl, combine the ground turkey, green onion tops, parsley, chives, salt, and pepper. Mix well.
- Form the mixture into four patties.
- Preheat the air fryer to 360°F (182°C).
- Place the patties in the air fryer basket and cook for about 10-12 minutes, flipping halfway through, or until the internal temperature reaches 165°F (74°C).
- Serve the burgers on gluten-free buns with lettuce, tomato, and mustard.

Health Benefits:

- Turkey is a lean protein source, helping to reduce fat intake while providing essential nutrients for muscle maintenance and overall health.
- Green onions, parsley, and chives add flavor without contributing high FODMAPs, making this meal ideal for digestive health.

Preparation Time: 20 minutes

4: Low FODMAP Air Fryer Stuffed Bell Peppers

Ingredients:

- 4 bell peppers, tops cut off and seeds removed
- 1 cup cooked quinoa
- 1/2 cup grated carrots
- 1/2 cup chopped tomatoes (seeded)
- 1/4 cup chopped fresh basil
- 1/4 cup crumbled feta cheese (lactose-free if needed)
- 2 tablespoons olive oil
- Salt and pepper, to taste

Instructions:

- In a bowl, mix together cooked quinoa, grated carrots, chopped tomatoes, fresh basil, crumbled feta, olive oil, salt, and pepper.
- Stuff each bell pepper with the quinoa mixture.
- Preheat the air fryer to 340°F (171°C).
- Place the stuffed peppers in the air fryer basket. Cook for about 10-15 minutes, or until the peppers are tender and the filling is heated through.

- Serve hot.

Health Benefits:

- Bell peppers are rich in vitamins A and C, which support immune function and skin health.
- Quinoa provides a complete protein source, containing all nine essential amino acids, while carrots and tomatoes add fiber and a variety of nutrients.
- This dish is well-rounded and filling, suitable for those on a Low FODMAP diet.

Preparation Time: 30 minutes

5: Low FODMAP Air Fryer Crispy Tofu

Ingredients:

- 1 block (14 oz) firm tofu, pressed and drained
- 1 tablespoon garlic-infused olive oil
- 1 tablespoon low-sodium soy sauce (or tamari for gluten-free option)
- 1 tablespoon cornstarch
- Salt and pepper, to taste

Instructions:

- Cut the tofu into 1-inch cubes.
- In a bowl, toss the tofu cubes with garlic-infused olive oil and soy sauce.
- Sprinkle cornstarch over the tofu and gently toss to coat evenly.
- Preheat the air fryer to 400°F (204°C).
- Arrange the tofu cubes in a single layer in the air fryer basket. Cook for 12-15 minutes, shaking the basket halfway through, until the tofu is golden brown and crispy.
- Season with salt and pepper to taste, and serve.

Health Benefits:

- Tofu is a great source of protein and contains all nine essential amino acids. It is also a valuable plant-based source of iron and calcium.
- The garlic-infused olive oil offers flavor without the high FODMAPs, making this dish beneficial for digestive health.

Preparation Time: 25 minutes

6: Low FODMAP Air Fryer Zucchini Chips

Ingredients:

- 2 medium zucchinis, thinly sliced
- 1 tablespoon olive oil
- 1/4 cup grated Parmesan cheese (ensure it's low-lactose if sensitive)
- Salt and pepper, to taste

Instructions:

- In a bowl, toss the thinly sliced zucchini with olive oil, Parmesan cheese, salt, and pepper.
- Preheat the air fryer to 375°F (190°C).
- Arrange the zucchini slices in a single layer in the air fryer basket. You may need to cook in batches to avoid overcrowding.
- Cook for 10-12 minutes, or until the zucchini chips are crispy and lightly browned.
- Serve immediately.

Health Benefits:

- Zucchini is low in calories but high in essential nutrients like potassium, manganese, and antioxidants like vitamin C and vitamin A.
- This recipe provides a healthy, crunchy snack or side dish that is easy on the stomach and low in FODMAPs.

Preparation Time: 20 minutes

7: Low FODMAP Air Fryer Maple Glazed Carrots

Ingredients:

- 4 large carrots, peeled and sliced diagonally
- 2 tablespoons olive oil
- 2 tablespoons pure maple syrup
- Salt and pepper, to taste
- Fresh parsley, chopped (for garnish)

Instructions:

- In a bowl, mix the olive oil and maple syrup together. Add the sliced carrots and toss to coat evenly.

- Preheat the air fryer to 380°F (193°C).
- Place the carrots in the air fryer basket, spreading them out evenly.
- Cook for 15-18 minutes, stirring halfway through, until the carrots are tender and caramelized.
- Season with salt and pepper to taste and garnish with fresh parsley before serving.

Health Benefits:

- Carrots are a great source of beta-carotene, fiber, vitamin K1, potassium, and antioxidants.
- They are low in FODMAPs and can help improve eye health and reduce the risk of chronic diseases.
- The addition of maple syrup provides a natural sweetness without using high FODMAP sweeteners.

Preparation Time: 25 minutes

8: Low FODMAP Air Fryer Lemon Pepper Shrimp

Ingredients:

- 1 pound shrimp, peeled and deveined
- 1 tablespoon garlic-infused olive oil

- 1 teaspoon lemon zest
- 1/2 teaspoon black pepper
- Lemon wedges, for serving

Instructions:

- In a bowl, toss the shrimp with garlic-infused olive oil, lemon zest, and black pepper.
- Preheat the air fryer to 400°F (204°C).
- Arrange the shrimp in a single layer in the air fryer basket.
- Cook for 6-8 minutes, or until the shrimp are pink and opaque.
- Serve immediately with lemon wedges on the side.

Health Benefits:

- Shrimp are a low-fat source of protein and provide important nutrients such as iodine, which is crucial for thyroid function and overall health.
- The lemon zest offers a boost of vitamin C and adds a fresh flavor, while the garlic-infused olive oil keeps it suitable for a Low FODMAP diet.

Preparation Time: 15 minutes

9: Low FODMAP Air Fryer Herb-Crusted Cod

Ingredients:

- 4 cod fillets (about 6 ounces each)
- 2 tablespoons garlic-infused olive oil
- 1/2 cup gluten-free breadcrumbs
- 2 tablespoons grated Parmesan cheese (low-lactose if sensitive)
- 1 teaspoon dried parsley
- 1 teaspoon dried dill
- Salt and pepper, to taste

Instructions:

- In a shallow bowl, combine the gluten-free breadcrumbs, Parmesan cheese, parsley, dill, salt, and pepper.
- Brush each cod fillet with garlic-infused olive oil and then dredge in the breadcrumb mixture until well coated.
- Preheat the air fryer to 400°F (204°C).

- Place the breaded cod fillets in the air fryer basket, ensuring they do not touch.
- Cook for 10-12 minutes, or until the cod is flaky and the crust is golden brown.
- Serve immediately, perhaps with a side of low FODMAP steamed vegetables.

Health Benefits:

- Cod is a low-fat source of high-quality protein and provides important vitamins and minerals, including B12, iodine, and selenium. This dish is low in FODMAPs, making it easy on the digestive system while providing a heart-healthy meal.

Preparation Time: 20 minutes

10: Low FODMAP Air Fryer Balsamic Chicken and Veggies

Ingredients:

- 4 chicken breasts, boneless and skinless
- 1 zucchini, sliced into half-moons
- 1 red bell pepper, seeded and chopped (if tolerated)
- 2 tablespoons balsamic vinegar

- 2 tablespoons garlic-infused olive oil
- 1 teaspoon dried basil
- Salt and pepper, to taste

Instructions:

- In a large bowl, combine balsamic vinegar, garlic-infused olive oil, basil, salt, and pepper.
- Add the chicken breasts and vegetables to the bowl and toss to coat.
- Preheat the air fryer to 360°F (182°C).
- Place the chicken and vegetables in the air fryer basket, arranging them in a single layer.
- Cook for 20-22 minutes, flipping the chicken halfway through and stirring the vegetables occasionally, until the chicken is cooked through and vegetables are tender.
- Serve hot.

Health Benefits:

- This recipe is excellent for those looking to maintain a balanced diet with high-quality protein from chicken and a good mix of vitamins and minerals from the vegetables.

- The use of garlic-infused olive oil and balsamic vinegar adds flavor without adding high FODMAP ingredients, supporting overall digestive health.

Preparation Time: 30 minutes

Low FODMAP Airfryer Dinner Recipes

1: Low FODMAP Air Fryer Garlic-Lime Tilapia

Ingredients:

- 4 tilapia fillets
- 2 tablespoons garlic-infused olive oil
- Juice of 1 lime
- 1 teaspoon dried parsley
- Salt and pepper, to taste
- Lime slices, for garnish

Instructions:

- In a small bowl, mix together the garlic-infused olive oil, lime juice, dried parsley, salt, and pepper.
- Brush each tilapia fillet with the mixture, ensuring both sides are well coated.

- Preheat the air fryer to 360°F (182°C).
- Place the tilapia fillets in the air fryer basket, ensuring they do not overlap.
- Cook for 10-12 minutes, or until the fish flakes easily with a fork.
- Serve the tilapia with additional lime slices for extra flavor.

Health Benefits:

- Tilapia is a low-fat source of protein and provides essential nutrients like omega-3 fatty acids, which are important for heart health and cognitive function.
- The garlic-infused olive oil offers flavor without adding FODMAPs, making this dish suitable for those with digestive sensitivities.

Preparation Time: 20 minutes

2: Low FODMAP Air Fryer Herb Roasted Chicken Thighs

Ingredients:

- 6 chicken thighs, bone-in and skin-on
- 2 tablespoons garlic-infused olive oil

- 1 teaspoon dried rosemary
- 1 teaspoon dried thyme
- Salt and pepper, to taste

Instructions:

- Rub each chicken thigh with garlic-infused olive oil.
- Sprinkle dried rosemary, thyme, salt, and pepper evenly over the chicken.
- Preheat the air fryer to 380°F (193°C).
- Arrange the chicken thighs in the air fryer basket, skin side up, making sure they do not touch each other.
- Cook for 25-30 minutes, or until the chicken is golden brown and the internal temperature reaches 165°F (74°C).
- Serve hot, garnished with fresh herbs if desired.

Health Benefits:

- Chicken thighs are a rich source of protein and also provide essential vitamins and minerals, including iron, selenium, and B vitamins.

- Cooking with herbs not only enhances flavor without the use of high FODMAP ingredients but also offers anti-inflammatory properties.

Preparation Time: 35 minutes

3: Low FODMAP Air Fryer Pork Tenderloin

Ingredients:

- 1 pork tenderloin (about 1 pound)
- 2 tablespoons garlic-infused olive oil
- 1 teaspoon dried oregano
- 1 teaspoon dried basil
- Salt and pepper, to taste

Instructions:

- Rub the pork tenderloin with garlic-infused olive oil.
- Season generously with dried oregano, basil, salt, and pepper.
- Preheat the air fryer to 400°F (204°C).
- Place the pork tenderloin in the air fryer basket.
- Cook for 20-25 minutes, or until the internal temperature reaches 145°F (63°C), flipping halfway through cooking.

- Let the pork rest for 5 minutes before slicing.
- Serve with a side of low FODMAP vegetables, such as green beans or a salad.

Health Benefits:

- Pork tenderloin is a lean protein source, essential for muscle repair and maintenance.
- The use of garlic-infused olive oil and herbs provides flavor without adding FODMAPs, promoting good digestion while enhancing the dish's taste.

Preparation Time: 30 minutes

4: Low FODMAP Air Fryer Maple-Glazed Salmon

Ingredients:

- 4 salmon fillets (about 6 ounces each)
- 2 tablespoons maple syrup
- 1 tablespoon garlic-infused olive oil
- 1 tablespoon Dijon mustard (ensure it's low FODMAP)
- Salt and pepper, to taste

Instructions:

- In a small bowl, mix together the maple syrup, garlic-infused olive oil, and Dijon mustard.
- Season the salmon fillets with salt and pepper.
- Brush the maple mixture over the salmon fillets.
- Preheat the air fryer to 400°F (204°C).
- Place the salmon fillets in the air fryer basket, skin side down.
- Cook for 7-10 minutes, or until the salmon is cooked through and flakes easily with a fork.
- Serve immediately, garnished with fresh herbs or lemon wedges if desired.

Health Benefits:

- Salmon is high in omega-3 fatty acids, which are crucial for heart health and reducing inflammation.
- The addition of maple syrup provides a natural sweetness without high FODMAP sugars, making this dish both delicious and gentle on the digestive system.

Preparation Time: 20 minutes

5: Low FODMAP Air Fryer Lemon Herb Flounder

Ingredients:

- 4 flounder fillets
- 2 tablespoons garlic-infused olive oil
- Juice of 1 lemon
- 1 teaspoon dried dill
- 1 teaspoon dried parsley
- Salt and pepper, to taste
- Lemon slices, for garnish

Instructions:

- In a small bowl, mix together the garlic-infused olive oil, lemon juice, dill, parsley, salt, and pepper.
- Lay the flounder fillets in a single layer and brush them with the lemon herb mixture.
- Preheat the air fryer to 360°F (182°C).
- Place the flounder fillets in the air fryer basket, making sure they do not overlap.
- Cook for 8-10 minutes, or until the fish is flaky and cooked through.

- Serve immediately, garnished with additional lemon slices.

Health Benefits:

- Flounder is a low-fat source of protein and provides B vitamins and phosphorus.
- The combination of lemon and herbs not only enhances flavor but also adds vitamin C and antioxidants without introducing high FODMAP ingredients, making this dish easy on the digestive system.

Preparation Time: 20 minutes

6: Low FODMAP Air Fryer Balsamic Glazed Eggplant

Ingredients:

- 2 medium eggplants, sliced into 1/2 inch rounds
- 3 tablespoons garlic-infused olive oil
- 3 tablespoons balsamic vinegar
- Salt and pepper, to taste
- Fresh basil, chopped for garnish

Instructions:

- In a large bowl, whisk together the garlic-infused olive oil, balsamic vinegar, salt, and pepper.
- Add the eggplant slices and toss to coat evenly.
- Preheat the air fryer to 375°F (190°C).
- Arrange the eggplant slices in a single layer in the air fryer basket, working in batches if necessary.
- Cook for 12-15 minutes, flipping halfway through, until the eggplant is tender and the edges are crispy.
- Serve hot, garnished with fresh basil.

Health Benefits:

- Eggplant is high in fiber and antioxidants, particularly nasunin found in the skin, which is known for its brain-protective properties.
- The use of garlic-infused olive oil and balsamic vinegar provides rich flavor without using high FODMAP ingredients, supporting overall gastrointestinal health.

Preparation Time: 30 minutes

7: Low FODMAP Air Fryer Stuffed Peppers

Ingredients:

- 4 bell peppers, tops cut off and seeded
- 1 cup cooked quinoa
- 1/2 cup chopped carrots
- 1/2 cup diced zucchini
- 1/4 cup chopped green onions (green parts only)
- 1 cup grated cheddar cheese (lactose-free if sensitive)
- 1 tablespoon garlic-infused olive oil
- Salt and pepper, to taste

Instructions:

- In a large bowl, mix the cooked quinoa, carrots, zucchini, green onions, half of the cheddar cheese, garlic-infused olive oil, salt, and pepper.
- Stuff each bell pepper with the quinoa mixture, packing it tightly.
- Top each pepper with the remaining cheddar cheese.
- Preheat the air fryer to 350°F (177°C).

- Place the stuffed peppers in the air fryer basket and cook for 15-20 minutes, or until the peppers are tender and the cheese is melted and bubbly.
- Serve hot.

Health Benefits:

- This meal is packed with vegetables, offering a good source of fiber, vitamins, and minerals.
- Quinoa provides a complete protein source, making this dish balanced in nutrients.
- The lactose-free cheese allows for dairy enjoyment without the discomfort, making this a hearty and healthy choice.

Preparation Time: 40 minutes

8: Low FODMAP Air Fryer Maple Dijon Chicken Drumsticks

Ingredients:

- 8 chicken drumsticks
- 2 tablespoons garlic-infused olive oil
- 3 tablespoons Dijon mustard (make sure it's low FODMAP)

- 2 tablespoons pure maple syrup
- 1 teaspoon dried thyme
- Salt and pepper, to taste

Instructions:

- In a small bowl, whisk together the garlic-infused olive oil, Dijon mustard, maple syrup, thyme, salt, and pepper.
- Coat the chicken drumsticks evenly with the maple Dijon mixture.
- Preheat the air fryer to 400°F (204°C).
- Arrange the chicken drumsticks in the air fryer basket.
- Cook for 25-30 minutes, turning halfway through, until the chicken is golden brown and cooked through.
- Serve hot.

Health Benefits:

- Chicken drumsticks are a good source of protein and essential minerals such as phosphorus, which helps with bone health.

- The combination of maple syrup and Dijon mustard provides a rich flavor without high FODMAP ingredients, making this dish both delicious and digestible.

Preparation Time: 40 minutes

9: Low FODMAP Air Fryer Lemon Pepper Cod

Ingredients:

- 4 cod fillets
- 2 tablespoons garlic-infused olive oil
- Juice and zest of 1 lemon
- 1 teaspoon black pepper
- Salt, to taste
- Fresh dill for garnish

Instructions:

- In a small bowl, mix the garlic-infused olive oil, lemon juice and zest, black pepper, and salt.
- Brush the mixture generously over the cod fillets.
- Preheat the air fryer to 360°F (182°C).
- Place the cod fillets in the air fryer basket, ensuring they do not overlap.

- Cook for 10-12 minutes or until the cod flakes easily with a fork.
- Garnish with fresh dill before serving.

Health Benefits:

- Cod is an excellent source of high-quality protein and omega-3 fatty acids, which are essential for heart and brain health.
- The lemon adds a good dose of vitamin C, enhancing immune function, while the use of garlic-infused oil keeps the dish low in FODMAPs, ensuring it's easy on the digestive system.

Preparation Time: 20 minutes

10: Low FODMAP Air Fryer Spiced Lamb Chops

Ingredients:

- 8 lamb chops
- 2 tablespoons garlic-infused olive oil
- 1 teaspoon dried rosemary
- 1 teaspoon dried thyme
- 1/2 teaspoon ground cumin

- Salt and pepper, to taste

Instructions:

- Rub each lamb chop with garlic-infused olive oil.
- Combine rosemary, thyme, cumin, salt, and pepper in a small bowl, then sprinkle the mixture over the lamb chops, ensuring even coverage.
- Preheat the air fryer to 400°F (204°C).
- Arrange the lamb chops in the air fryer basket in a single layer.
- Cook for 10-14 minutes, turning halfway through, or until the lamb reaches your desired doneness.
- Serve hot, perhaps with a side of low FODMAP vegetables.

Health Benefits:

- Lamb is a rich source of high-quality protein and vital nutrients like iron, zinc, and B vitamins, which are important for energy metabolism and overall health.
- The herbs used in this recipe provide antioxidants without high FODMAPs, making this dish flavorful and digestive-friendly.

Preparation Time: 25 minutes

Low FODMAP Airfryer Snacks Recipes

1: Low FODMAP Air Fryer Plantain Chips

Ingredients:

- 2 green plantains
- 1 tablespoon garlic-infused olive oil
- Salt, to taste

Instructions:

- Peel the plantains and slice them thinly, ideally using a mandoline slicer for uniform thickness.
- Toss the plantain slices in garlic-infused olive oil to lightly coat them.
- Sprinkle with salt.
- Preheat the air fryer to 360°F (182°C).
- Arrange the plantain slices in a single layer in the air fryer basket. You may need to cook them in batches to avoid overcrowding.
- Cook for 10-15 minutes, flipping the chips halfway through, until they are golden brown and crispy.

- Let them cool slightly before serving to enhance their crispiness.

Health Benefits:

- Plantains are a good source of vitamins A and C, potassium, and dietary fiber, which supports digestive health.
- Cooking them in an air fryer with garlic-infused olive oil provides a delicious snack with minimal fat, suitable for the Low FODMAP diet.

Preparation Time: 20 minutes

2: Low FODMAP Air Fryer Parmesan Zucchini Bites

Ingredients:

- 2 medium zucchinis, cut into 1/2-inch slices
- 1/4 cup grated Parmesan cheese (low-lactose if sensitive)
- 1 tablespoon olive oil
- Salt and pepper, to taste

Instructions:

- In a bowl, toss the zucchini slices with olive oil, and season with salt and pepper.
- Arrange the zucchini slices in a single layer in the air fryer basket.
- Sprinkle grated Parmesan cheese evenly over the zucchini slices.
- Preheat the air fryer to 380°F (193°C).
- Cook for 8-10 minutes, or until the zucchini is tender and the Parmesan is golden and crispy.
- Serve immediately.

Health Benefits:

- Zucchini is low in calories and high in essential nutrients like vitamin C, vitamin A, and potassium, which aid in maintaining a healthy heart and strong vision.
- Parmesan adds a flavorful touch along with calcium and protein. This snack is Low FODMAP friendly, making it easy to digest while satisfying hunger.

Preparation Time: 15 minutes

3: Low FODMAP Air Fryer Sweet Potato Fries

Ingredients:

- 2 large sweet potatoes, peeled and cut into fries
- 2 tablespoons garlic-infused olive oil
- 1 teaspoon smoked paprika
- Salt, to taste

Instructions:

- Toss the sweet potato fries with garlic-infused olive oil and smoked paprika in a bowl. Season with salt.
- Preheat the air fryer to 380°F (193°C).
- Arrange the fries in a single layer in the air fryer basket. You may need to cook in batches to avoid overcrowding, which can affect crispiness.
- Cook for 15-20 minutes, shaking the basket halfway through, until the fries are crispy and golden.
- Serve immediately.

Health Benefits:

- Sweet potatoes are a fantastic source of dietary fiber, vitamins A and C, and potassium. These nutrients support vision health, immune function, and digestive health. The use of garlic-infused olive oil adds flavor without adding FODMAPs, making these fries a hearty and healthy snack option.

Preparation Time: 25 minutes

4: Low FODMAP Air Fryer Crispy Chickpeas

Ingredients:

- 1 can (15 oz) chickpeas, rinsed and thoroughly dried
- 1 tablespoon garlic-infused olive oil
- 1 teaspoon ground cumin
- Salt, to taste

Instructions:

- Toss the dried chickpeas with garlic-infused olive oil, cumin, and salt in a bowl.
- Preheat the air fryer to 390°F (200°C).
- Spread the chickpeas in a single layer in the air fryer basket.

- Cook for 12-15 minutes, shaking the basket every few minutes, until the chickpeas are golden and crispy.
- Let them cool slightly before serving to enhance their crispness.

Health Benefits:

- Chickpeas are a great source of protein and fiber, which promote satiety and aid in digestive health.
- The garlic-infused olive oil and cumin provide a flavorful kick without including high FODMAP ingredients, making these chickpeas a perfect, crunchy snack.

Preparation Time: 20 minutes

5: Low FODMAP Air Fryer Mozzarella Sticks

Ingredients:

- 8 mozzarella sticks (ensure they're low-lactose if sensitive)
- 1/2 cup gluten-free breadcrumbs
- 1/4 cup grated Parmesan cheese (low-lactose if sensitive)

- 1 teaspoon dried oregano
- 1 egg, beaten
- Salt and pepper, to taste

Instructions:

- Freeze the mozzarella sticks for at least an hour before cooking.
- In a shallow bowl, mix the gluten-free breadcrumbs, grated Parmesan, dried oregano, salt, and pepper.
- Dip each frozen mozzarella stick first into the beaten egg, then roll in the breadcrumb mixture until well coated. Repeat this step for a double layer of coating for extra crunch.
- Preheat the air fryer to 400°F (204°C).
- Place the coated mozzarella sticks in the air fryer basket, making sure they do not touch each other.
- Cook for 6-8 minutes, or until the exterior is golden and crispy.
- Serve immediately with a low FODMAP marinara sauce.

Health Benefits:

- Mozzarella sticks provide a good source of calcium and protein. Using low-lactose cheese makes this snack easier to digest for those with lactose intolerance.
- The gluten-free coating ensures the snack is safe for those with gluten sensitivities.

Preparation Time: About 1 hour and 20 minutes (including freezing time)

6: Low FODMAP Air Fryer Kale Chips

Ingredients:

- 1 bunch of kale, leaves torn into bite-sized pieces (stems removed)
- 1 tablespoon olive oil
- Salt, to taste

Instructions:

- Wash and thoroughly dry the kale leaves.
- In a large bowl, toss the kale with olive oil and salt until evenly coated.
- Preheat the air fryer to 375°F (190°C).

- Spread the kale in a single layer in the air fryer basket. You may need to do this in batches to avoid overcrowding.
- Cook for 4-6 minutes, or until the kale chips are crispy and slightly browned at the edges.
- Serve immediately for best texture.

Health Benefits:

- Kale is a nutritional powerhouse, packed with vitamins A, K, and C, as well as antioxidants and fiber, which support overall health and digestion.
- Making kale chips in the air fryer uses minimal oil, making this a low-calorie, nutrient-dense snack that fits perfectly into a Low FODMAP diet.

Preparation Time: 15 minutes

7: Low FODMAP Air Fryer Cinnamon Banana Chips

Ingredients:

- 2 firm bananas
- 1 teaspoon cinnamon
- 1 tablespoon coconut oil, melted

Instructions:

- Slice the bananas into thin chips.
- In a small bowl, mix the melted coconut oil and cinnamon.
- Toss the banana slices in the cinnamon oil to coat them evenly.
- Preheat the air fryer to 350°F (177°C).
- Arrange the banana chips in a single layer in the air fryer basket. You may need to cook in batches to avoid overcrowding.
- Cook for 10-12 minutes or until the banana chips are crispy and golden brown, flipping them halfway through the cooking time.
- Allow the chips to cool to further crisp up before serving.

Health Benefits:

- Bananas are a good source of potassium and vitamins, and when cooked, they provide a healthy, sweet snack without the need for added sugars.
- Cinnamon adds anti-inflammatory properties and can help regulate blood sugar levels. Coconut oil

provides a medium-chain fatty acid that supports metabolism.

Preparation Time: 20 minutes

8: Low FODMAP Air Fryer Polenta Fries

Ingredients:

- 1 tube of pre-cooked polenta, cut into fries
- 2 tablespoons olive oil
- 1 teaspoon salt
- 1/2 teaspoon pepper
- 1/2 teaspoon paprika (optional)

Instructions:

- Preheat the air fryer to 400°F (204°C).
- Toss the polenta fries with olive oil, salt, pepper, and paprika in a bowl.
- Arrange the fries in a single layer in the air fryer basket. Cook in batches if necessary to avoid overcrowding.
- Cook for 15-20 minutes, shaking the basket halfway through, until the fries are crispy and golden.

- Serve hot, with a side of low FODMAP friendly dipping sauce if desired.

Health Benefits:

- Polenta is a good source of carbohydrates and fiber, providing a steady energy release. It is naturally gluten-free, making it a great option for those with gluten intolerance or celiac disease.
- The olive oil adds healthy fats, which are essential for nutrient absorption.

Preparation Time: 30 minutes

9: Low FODMAP Air Fryer Carrot Fries

Ingredients:

- 4 large carrots, peeled and cut into sticks
- 1 tablespoon olive oil
- 1/2 teaspoon dried thyme
- Salt and pepper, to taste

Instructions:

- Toss the carrot sticks with olive oil, dried thyme, salt, and pepper in a bowl until evenly coated.

- Preheat the air fryer to 380°F (193°C).
- Arrange the carrot sticks in a single layer in the air fryer basket. You might need to do this in batches to avoid overcrowding.
- Cook for 15-20 minutes, shaking the basket halfway through, until the carrots are tender and slightly crispy.
- Serve warm as a healthy snack.

Health Benefits:

- Carrots are rich in beta-carotene, fiber, vitamin K, potassium, and antioxidants, which support vision health, digestive health, and immune function. Using olive oil adds healthy fats, enhancing nutrient absorption without irritating the gut.

Preparation Time: 25 minutes

10: Low FODMAP Air Fryer Stuffed Mushrooms

Ingredients:

- 12 large button mushrooms, stems removed

- 1/4 cup finely chopped green onion (green parts only)
- 1/4 cup grated Parmesan cheese (low-lactose if sensitive)
- 1 tablespoon garlic-infused olive oil
- Salt and pepper, to taste

Instructions:

- Preheat the air fryer to 350°F (177°C).
- In a small bowl, combine the green onion, Parmesan cheese, garlic-infused olive oil, salt, and pepper.
- Fill each mushroom cap with the mixture.
- Arrange the stuffed mushrooms in the air fryer basket, ensuring they are not overcrowded.
- Cook for 8-10 minutes or until the mushrooms are tender and the filling is golden brown.
- Serve hot, garnished with additional green onions if desired.

Health Benefits:

- Mushrooms are a good source of protein, fiber, and antioxidants without the addition of high FODMAP ingredients. They provide selenium, potassium, and B vitamins.

- The garlic-infused olive oil and Parmesan offer a flavor boost while keeping the dish suitable for a Low FODMAP diet.

Preparation Time: 20 minutes

CONCLUSION

This Low FODMAP Air Fryer Cookbook offers a robust collection of recipes designed to bring ease, flavor, and health to your daily meals.

Each recipe has been carefully crafted to ensure it meets Low FODMAP standards, providing relief and comfort for those with sensitive digestive systems without sacrificing taste or satisfaction.

The air fryer, a remarkable tool for health-conscious cooks, allows you to enjoy your favorite dishes with less oil and fat, making each meal not only easier to digest but also heart-healthy.

From crispy snacks and hearty breakfasts to nutritious lunches and delightful dinners, this cookbook demonstrates that following a Low FODMAP diet does not mean depriving yourself of delicious food. Instead, it opens up a new realm of culinary creativity and flavor exploration, all while keeping your health and wellness in check.

Whether you're a seasoned chef or new to the kitchen, these recipes provide simple, straightforward instructions to ensure success.

Embrace the journey of Low FODMAP cooking with your air fryer and rediscover the joy of eating well. Let this cookbook be your guide to a happier, healthier gut and a more joyful, flavorful life.

Enjoy the process, delight in each meal, and celebrate the benefits that come with taking care of your digestive health through thoughtful, delicious food choices.

Printed in Great Britain
by Amazon